BERNICE PIER

JUNE

CASSOPOLIS, M

D0990955

Pottery Throwing for Beginners

Pottery throwing for beginners

Kenneth Clark

Studio Vista London
Watson-Guptill Publications New York

Acknowledgements

The author would like to thank most sincerely Mr Howard Williams for his help and co-operation in taking the photographs; all those whose work has been used to illustrate this book; Ann Herschman for typing the text; and above all the editor and designer at Studio Vista for their patience and constant help.

General editors Janey O'Riordan and Brenda Herbert
© Kenneth Clark 1970
Published in London by Studio Vista Limited
Blue Star House, Highgate Hill, London N19
and in New York by Watson-Guptill Publications
165 West 46th Street, New York 10036
Library of Congress Catalog Card Number 76-99932
Set in 9 on 9½pt Univers
Printed and bound in Great Britain by
Bookprint Limited, Crawley, Sussex
SBN 289.79755.1

Contents

1 About throwing

Pots were hand built for centuries before they were thrown on the first wheels somewhere around 3,000 years or more B.C. In technique, it was a natural progression to a faster revolving lump of clay being squeezed and formed into shape by the hands of the thrower. At particular periods in history pots were made for purely decorative purposes, but the bulk of all thrown ware has been for man's use, produced in a rural environment to supply local needs. At some periods it did develop literally into areas of industry, where the wares were exported to distant markets, as in the case of ancient Greek pottery, which found its way to many Mediterranean capitals.

It was not until the Industrial Revolution in England, and the technological approach of Josiah Wedgwood, that the task of supplying man's ceramic needs was transferred from country craftsmen to industrial craftsmen and operatives. This change was so thorough in England that, by the early 20th century, there was only a handful of country potteries still in operation whose production stemmed from articles thrown on the wheel. The strong influence of Bernard Leech and his followers on our modern studio pottery movement grew from wheel-thrown pottery and an awareness of the variable qualities of different clay bodies and the results they produced when fired.

There are still potters who believe throwing to be the mainspring of ceramic expression, and who rather overlook the fact that a great deal of the world's superb pottery was produced before the wheel was invented, or without its aid. There is no doubt, however, that even from the earliest examples one can discern a quality that is unique to throwing, ranging from a direct, earthy spontaneity to a superb, controlled subtlety.

Throwing in this century has changed from a functional production technique to a more conscious vehicle for artistic expression. In the past few years there has been a movement by certain craftsmen potters to produce predominantly domestic ware which is often cheaper than good quality industrial pottery. This has only been achieved by working mainly in the country, where it is possible to keep overheads to an absolute minimum. At the same time, throwing for some potters has become more a means to an end than an end in itself. Some have thrown shapes which have been cut when leather-hard to be re-assembled as intricate and beautifully balanced structures with a predominantly sculptural quality. Others have used the technique to develop ideas and shapes that have eventually been translated into forms for industrial production, both purely decorative and as domestic ware.

Fig 1   A group of thrown prototype shapes that are intended to be made finally in a factory. In this case, throwing is used in a design context, as a means to an end

There is little that throwing has not been subjected to experimentally, and it is said that some time ago in America some students attached a fixed wheel to a ceiling and threw pots downwards rather than upwards.

Throwing has something of magic in it. The unbelievable happens before your eyes. A wet lump of clay spins rapidly on the wheel-head and appears to change shape and grow with ease under the firm pressure of the hands. It is fascinating and completely absorbing for both thrower and spectator.

If your enthusiasm and desire are strong enough, you can learn to throw; all beginners make mistakes, but these can be corrected with practice, so there is no need to be discouraged if your first efforts are disappointing. I have thrown for years and it still gives me great personal pleasure, and I can still remember the thrill and sense of achievement in throwing my first pots. Practically no other craft gives one such an immediate sense of fulfilment as that of throwing a pot.

As with all skills, 'practice makes perfect', but for those who eventually aspire to more than competence, high standards of an aesthetic nature must also be encouraged. One recognizes good throwing instinctively, just as one is drawn to the playing of an instrument by someone who is more than just a good instrumentalist.

For those who intend to make ceramics a career, the ability to throw well with a natural rhythm does enrich their sensibilities and command of clay as a material. Good throwing achieves certain qualities that are not possible by hand building techniques and are a synthesis of more direct and rapid handling, fusing skill and concept. As with all hand skills, it is essential to have good personal tuition to complement whatever may be written about the subject. Most difficulties are more imagined than real, so that a carefree, optimistic attitude to throwing is a great help.

2 Clay: uses and preparation

Personalities differ, and so do clays, and, like personalities, some clays are more popular for obvious logical reasons. Clays can be chosen to suit the user's tastes, as long as they do the job that is required of them.

Types of clay

RED EARTHENWARE CLAY

There is a plentiful supply of good, plastic red clay in most parts of the world, but not all of this is used for throwing. Some countries use it mainly for roof tiles, bricks, pipes and floor tiles, often with the addition of sand to reduce shrinkage and excess plasticity.

Red clays are cheaper and more easily obtainable than white clays, and therefore more suitable for beginners. Because of the average metallic iron content of the red clays (approximately 8%) their firing temperature is limited, because the iron oxide begins to fuse and help melt the clay body at temperatures beyond 1100°C (2012°F). They are therefore strictly earthenware clays, and can vitrify as low as 980°–1000°C (1796°–1832°F). Vitrification takes place when the clay begins to melt and becomes a glassy mass, and is no longer porous.

WHITE CLAYS

The purest form of clay is china clay which has never moved from its original forming ground. It is therefore called a *primary clay*, but unfortunately it is not plastic.

Ball clays are called *secondary clays*. These are comparatively pure, white plastic clays which have become plastic in the journey from their forming grounds over vast periods of time. Some are excessively plastic and need the addition of other raw materials to reduce their plasticity, and this often increases the maturing or vitrifying temperature (see chapter 8).

Clays are therefore broadly classified as *earthenware*, *stoneware* and *porcelain*. Most earthenware clays are red, and fire from 980°–1100°C (1796°–2012°F); white earthenware clays fire from 1060°–1150°C (1940°–2102°F); all of these are porous. Stoneware clays are mainly white to grey, non-porous, and fire from 1200°–1300°C (2192°–2372°F). Porcelain clays are whitish-grey, non-porous, and sometimes translucent, and fire from 1280°–1350°C (2336°–2460°F).

Preparing a clay sample

It is much more convenient to buy a satisfactory, clean, prepared throwing clay than to dig and prepare your own. However, great pleasure can be got from finding and preparing a perfectly adequate throwing clay found in its natural state. In fact, in some countries this is the only way to procure your clay. This may be done in two ways.

The first and most thorough method is to dig the clay and let it dry out thoroughly. Then place a given quantity in a shallow container, after having broken it up into small pieces, and just cover it with water and let it stand. After 40−60 minutes the water will have completely broken down the clay and it may then be stirred and sieved easily through an 80 mesh sieve. Observe what foreign matter, coarse sand, or pebbles, may have been retained, and if this is not more than about 10 per cent of the original weight, dry out the slip on a plaster bat or slab till in a consistent throwing state. Roll a 12-inch coil about the thickness of the thumb and allow it to dry slowly, and when bone dry measure the shrinkage. Fire to normal earthenware temperature (see above), and again measure the shrinkage. If the total shrinkage is not more than 10 per cent it may be a satisfactory throwing clay, provided it has the required plasticity and provided that you have test-thrown a piece and have carried out a limited number of glaze tests on it.

The second and quicker method is to dig the clay, knead it by hand (when you can directly feel its composition) and, when well mixed, carry out a shrinkage test and throw a number of small articles with it. Most traditional country potters did just this and you can often still see small pebbles embedded in the ware as a result. It is only when you require a more sophisticated studio pot that you should take more trouble with the cleaning and preparation of the clay.

Some clays can be dug and used immediately, and others should be weathered or kept moist for long periods before use. This can only be discovered by experiment. If the same clay is used over and over again when practising throwing it becomes tired and overworked, and needs to be left for some time before being used again. This of course never happens in a working pottery, as articles are made directly with the clay and are immediately translated into a finished ceramic article.

Suitable prepared clay may be stored for long periods wrapped in a plastic sheet, but even this does not indefinitely retain all the moisture (see page 92).

Preparing clay for throwing

A good potter is a thorough potter, and the thorough mixing or wedging of his clay, to give it the same consistency throughout, is of the utmost importance.

If you throw with clay which is too moist it will not support the shape, or stand being thrown thinly. Alternatively, if it is too hard or stiff it will be difficult to centre and will need so much pressure when being thinned or shaped that the article will twist and possibly collapse. As a rule, the softer the clay, the quicker it must be handled and the quicker it responds to pressure. Harder clay will need slower handling and more pressure.

The clay itself must have sufficient plasticity to be easily handled and keep the shape required, but not so plastic that it is sticky. It should not have too critical a water absorption level (the point at which certain clays can suddenly become very soft and lose their flexibility with even a slight increase in water), and from the thrown state to dry clay, it should have between 8 per cent and 10 per cent shrinkage.

THE DIFFERENT STATES OF CLAY

Naturally dug clay is rather crumbly when dry, and very close and cake-like in texture when damp.

Plastic clay ready for throwing is like firm dough, not sticky, and easily squeezed.

Slip is any clay mixed with water to an even texture with the consistency of thick to medium cream.

Leather-hard clay has the consistency of a firm cheese, is slightly soft when pressed with the finger nail, and is easily cut with a knife but difficult to cut with a wire or nylon thread.

Bone dry, or white hard, clay is when it has been completely air-dried and all moisture has evaporated, leaving it hard and brittle.

WEDGING

Almost every movement in throwing is some form of squeezing the clay, and for it to respond evenly to pressure it must be absolutely evenly mixed throughout. Wedging is the technique of mixing or kneading moist clay by hand to achieve this even consistency. There are several methods of wedging, but the simplest is to use a rhythmic movement very similar to the way in which a baker kneads his dough. The consistency of the clay must be thoroughly checked before use. To do this, cut the lump of clay

Fig 2   Drawings showing clay cut into layers, placed on edge, and then flattened and re-wedged

with wire or nylon thread at several levels, as in fig. 2. Observe how even the texture is, or draw the finger across the cut surface so that any variations in texture can immediately be felt. If the result is not satisfactory, wedging must be repeated.

KEEPING CLAY MOIST

Whenever possible, prepare your clay and use it as soon as possible. If left uncovered even for a short while, the outer surfaces begin to dry as the moisture evaporates. At the same time, if the clay is placed on any absorbent material, such as wood, or plaster, the moisture will be absorbed, soon leaving the area in contact drier and harder than the rest of the clay.

Draughts will dry clay and pots quicker than heat, but this can be an advantage in drying pots if organized with care.

However thorough one is in trying to keep clay wrapped and soft the tendency is for it eventually to dry out. Therefore, as a general rule, any clay that has been damped or mixed for re-use is best lightly mixed in too soft a state for throwing, wrapped in plastic and, when needed, wedged to the desired consistency on an absorbent surface.

Clay which has become too hard may be softened by wrapping it with a very wet cloth and then rolling in a thick plastic bag. The moisture will in time penetrate the clay, and a quick wedge should soon have it ready for use, providing the ball of clay is not very large.

OVER-SOFT CLAY

Fine sand or grog (ground pots that have been fired once) may be added to excessively plastic clays, but if it is too coarse it will naturally hurt the hands. This addition of sand reduces the plasticity, increases the firing temperature, and reduces the shrinkage and tendency to warp excessively in drying, particularly if tiles or large containers are being made from the clay.

The best method of mixing sand with clay is to begin with over-soft clay, wedging it against a pile of the required quantity of sand on the bench. At each revolution of the clay, the sand will adhere to it, and so become evenly distributed throughout the mass.

3 The basic technique

Throwing is primarily a skill, which can be learnt by most people. For some it is an easy and natural process, but for others it may be a difficult and slow task.

Whether you wish to become a productive craftsman or an artist craftsman, you must be able to manipulate the clay with confidence. Thrown pots made with few and simple movements have a directness and spontaneity, essential to good throwing. These qualities should be a constant objective when practising all forms of throwing.

You must be single-minded and ruthless from the very beginning, accepting no second-best. You should never attempt to save a pot when it is clear that something has gone wrong. Better to discard the clay and begin again. Should you find that you keep making a particular mistake, refer to the section dealing with basic faults in throwing on page 60.

If possible, you should have a clear mental picture of what you intend to make and the movements you will use to achieve it.

Beginning to throw

One of the most important things is the way you move when throwing. While centering, your arms may rest on the edge of the throwing tray; but all throwing movements should be controlled by freely pivoting arms or elbows, keeping them close to the body for maximum effort, rather as a boxer moves. Keep as close as is comfortably possible to your pot.

Place a round ball of prepared clay firmly in the centre of the wheel-head and set it rapidly in motion (fig. 3). The size of the clay lump should fit comfortably between both hands and can be larger as your skill improves.

Fig 3   Placing a ball of clay on the wheel-head ready for centering. This is a suitable-sized ball of clay for beginners

Fig 4   Centering the ball of clay. Note elbow tucked into thigh, and forearm and wrist straight for maximum effect

Fig 5 Squeezing the clay into a cone shape with the palms of both hands. Note angle of left palm and ball of thumb determining slope of cone

Fig 6 Flattening the cone with palms and ball of both thumbs. Lower area of palm contains the shape and keeps the clay domed

Fig 7 Alternative method, flattening cone of clay with two hands interlocked. Right hand pressing downwards and left palm containing the clay by inward pressure

Fig 8   Thumb stiff and making dent in the dome of clay while fingers act as steadying guide, touching edge of clay

Fig 9   Wrist raised, with thumb and fingers held rigid as thumb presses firmly downwards ready to open out to form inside base of pot

Fig 10   Cross section showing thumb ready to press horizontally outwards and being steadied by finger held firmly against outer edge of clay ball

The right hand overlaps the left and exerts pressure with the palm (fig. 4). Keeping the palms vertical, press inwards until the clay rises into a cone shape (fig. 5).

Now press downwards with the thumbs and palms (fig. 6), or with the fleshy portion of the right hand, with the palm of the left hand counter-balancing the outward thrust of the clay (fig. 7).

Repeat this movement several times until the dome-shaped clay is felt to spin evenly at the centre of the wheel-head. This is called *centering*.

Now with right thumb stiff and fingers braced to the side of the spinning clay, slowly make a dent with the thumb (fig. 8) and at the same time raise the wrist, pressing downwards (fig. 9) until the point of the thumb is approximately $\frac{1}{2}$ in. from the wheel-head (fig. 10).

With the left hand firmly supporting the fingers of the right hand (fig. 11), press away from the body horizontally with the thumb, leaving a flat area inside the clay (fig. 12).

Retaining the position shown in fig. 12 and using mainly the right thumb and fingers, draw the clay upwards and inwards, relaxing the pressure only when nearing the top of the cylinder (figs 13 and 14). You now have a thick cylinder with vertical inside wall and the outside wall sloping towards the top. The top edge of the cylinder should never be made too thin in the early stages.

The thicker clay at the base must now be lifted and distributed evenly into the walls of the cylinder so that it grows taller but not wider. To do this, place the fingers of the left hand together inside the pot at the base (point *a*, fig. 15), and at the same time press directly inwards with the clenched first finger and thumb of the right hand. The right knuckle is now under the thickness of clay and ready to press inwards and upwards till above the inside fingers (fig. 16) which firmly resist the pressure and lift and squeeze the clay up into the walls of the cylinder.

This is repeated till the thicker clay at the base of the cylinder is evenly distributed (fig. 17). The walls should now be consistently even in thickness. Depending on the size of the cylinder, this should seldom take more than three knucklings. Sufficient thickness should be left on the wheel-head to allow for cutting off the pot and for turning a foot-ring.

In throwing, the pressure should always be greatest where the clay is thickest. As thinner areas are reached the pressure with the fingers is automatically reduced.

As a general rule, the wheel should run comparatively fast when

Fig 11   Left hand firmly supports right hand as thumb opens out centered clay to form inside base

Fig 12   Sectional view with inside base shaped and bulk of clay ready to be squeezed and lifted upwards with right hand, still controlled and guided by left hand

Fig 13   Squeezing and lifting clay in walls of thick cylinder

Fig 14   Finishing thick cylinder with inside wall about vertical and sloping outside profile

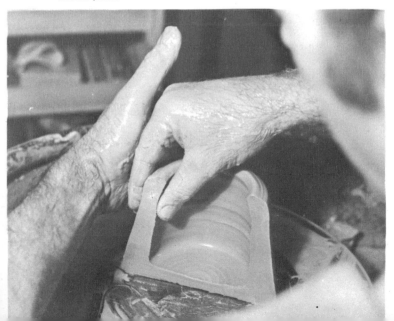

Fig 15   First stage of knuckling, with the right fingers pressing inwards to be under the thickness of clay and ready to push upwards till above the left fingers, which then resist pressure and lift the clay from the inside

Fig 16   Right hand clenched, knuckles pressing inwards, and left-hand fingers lifting and squeezing the clay upwards and thinning the wall of the pot

Fig 17   Cross-section of a standard cylinder showing even thickness of walls and
thicker base to allow for turning foot-ring

Fig 18   First finger of right hand pressing to keep top edge of cylinder level, and
thumb and forefinger of left hand firmly supporting top edge and resisting
outward pressures

Fig 19   Levelling top of pot and shaping neck prior to shaping the body of the pot as in fig. 20. Note pressure of top edge of pot between third and little finger.

centering, and as the pot or clay becomes thinner the speed should be gradually reduced. For the final shaping, particularly of a bowl or large pot, the wheel needs to run as slow as possible, in fact almost to the point of stopping.

The surface of the clay should be kept slippery, by dipping the hands in water from time to time. Occasionally the pot may also be splashed with water during throwing. Practised throwers use very little water, but this is only possible when pots are thrown quickly. If too much water is used, the pot becomes waterlogged and may collapse. A natural sponge is the most suitable for use when throwing. If excess water accumulates in a tall cylinder or pot it can be soaked up with a sponge tied to the end of a stick.

At every stage of throwing the top edge of the article should be kept level, and this is achieved by firm support with the left forefinger and thumb, and a steady downward pressure with the first finger of the right hand (fig. 18). Another excellent technique is to support the outer edge of the cylinder with the left hand and hold and press downwards, with the top edge held between the fingers of the right hand (fig. 19). At the same time the right hand can shape the top of the pot, or reduce the aperture by working closely with the left hand squeezing the neck in, varying the shape by altering the angle of the right hand and fingers.

Shaping a pot after having made a cylinder is done by pressing or squeezing the clay from either the inside or outside of the pot. The pressure will naturally vary, but the correct distance between the hands, or fingers of each hand, must be maintained to ensure the correct thickness of the pot's walls. Most shaping is done with an outward pressure of the fingers of the left hand, which are inside the pot (fig. 20). However, by pressing inwards and resisting the outward thrust of the clay in motion, the right hand can

Fig 20 Shaping cylinder with the flat edge of inside fingers and right hand
knuckle, to form a full shape

shape the clay inwards (fig. 21), the fingers of both hands working together all the time with varying pressures when needed. When shaping inwards, the inside fingers are higher than the outside knuckles.

The final operation is to remove the pot either by sliding or lifting it off the wheel-head. To slide off, put some water on the wheel-head and draw it under the pot by cutting with a piece of nylon thread or twisted wire stretched between the ends of the thumbs; and then slide the pot off onto the hand as in figs 22 and 23. Fig. 24 shows the method of lowering the pot onto a board.

To lift off a tall shape, trim away the thin layer of wet clay near the base with a turning tool (see page 40), cut off with dry wire or nylon thread, and with dry hands tilt the pot and, at the same time, lift it from wheel-head. This may be done with either the fingers or the hands according to the size of the pot (fig. 26).

Fig 21   Shaping the neck inwards, with inside fingers higher than outside

Fig 22   Sliding a bowl onto the right hand held level with edge of wheel-head

Fig 23   Plan view of fig. 22

Fig 24   Lowering bowl gently onto board and sliding fingers away

Fig 25 Selection of medieval jugs with applied decoration

Fig 26   Placing a stemmed shape on a board after lifting from the wheel. The pot has been held firmly with dry hands and the surface of pot is sticky but not slippery

There are several techniques of throwing, but all are based on the same principle of pressing and squeezing the clay. The more direct, simple and economic the movements you use, the more satisfactory your throwing technique will become. This can be checked by a careful and logical assessment of what you have been practising.

Throwing should be practised in three stages—centering, making a cylinder, and then shaping from a cylinder. Each stage should be practised continuously until you have mastered it with confidence, before going on to the next one; the three stages should eventually become a continuous operation.

4 Making and turning

Fig 27 Knuckling up a beaker. Note angle of right hand to pot, and relationship of both hands

Fig 28 Using the tips of the fingers to shape, gently but firmly, the profile of a beaker

Having practised the very basic techniques of throwing till you can almost do them with your eyes shut (and this is worth trying), the next step is to learn to vary the technique in order to make a wider range of shapes.

The logical development from the cylinder is a beaker shape (fig. 27), with sides sloping slightly outwards. This may sound simple, but a very subtle increase of pressure is needed, otherwise the top will flare out into a curved rather than a straight profile.

The first outward shaping may be done with finger and knuckles (fig. 27), the second and more gentle adjustments with the tips of the fingers of both hands working in unison (fig. 28).

There are many variations on an oval shape (fig. 29), which again needs firm but gentle handling to retain this simple but subtle form. When determining the inside of the base, give it sufficient width to be stable. Keep the inside corners crisp, and not curved, otherwise the base will become too heavy at the edges (fig. 30). A common fault is to continue shaping outwards

Fig 30   Cross section, showing position of hands when shaping an oval pot, and indicating position when fingers become level, and then change over with inside fingers becoming higher

for too long, ending up with a short fat pot. When making an oval shape you should begin to reverse the shaping at least half way up the pot (fig. 30), as it is easier to extend the shape with the finger tips only, once the initial knuckling has been carried out.

Do not let the neck of the pot get too wide, but after each shaping which necessitates the insertion of the left hand, squeeze it in to reduce the diameter (fig. 19) until the neck has been finally shaped.

A spherical shape (fig. 31 a–f) is perhaps the most difficult to throw because the clay has to be evenly distributed in opposite directions, inwards at the top and far out at the middle. Careful calculation is necessary to leave sufficient clay for the top half of the pot and not use it all up making the belly of the shape. Here one needs to learn and practice how to thin and shape the clay at the same time in order to disperse it more evenly. As with most shapes, the shaping of the bottom half of the pot should be completed first, and then the top half finished. This should all be

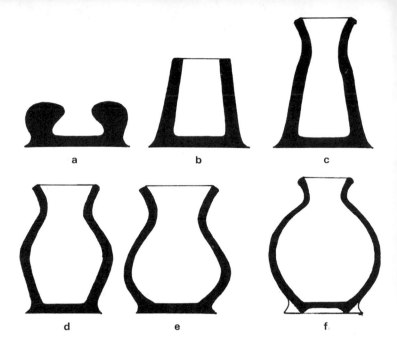

a   b   c

d   e   f

Fig 31   Drawings showing the stages in throwing a round pot

done as quickly and correctly as possible, otherwise the clay becomes too thin, tired, and possibly soft with water, and is then
liable to collapse. The neck of a sphere should be well supported
inside with the left fingers when shaping, as the tendency is for
the shoulder of the pot to twist due to insufficient support and
the clay becoming too thin.

It is from stage d to e that one has to thin and shape the sphere.
When making a sphere, always keep in mind that it is the inside
shape that will determine the final profile, which will subsequently
be defined by any necessary turning that may be done. A common
fault is to end up with what looks like a collapsing sphere,
because the pot has been thrown by concentrating on the
profile and not the inside shape.

For all bowls you must start with a different technique from
that used when making a cylinder. After centering the clay and
inserting the thumb, begin immediately to create the basic form
and direction that the particular bowl will eventually take (fig.32).
The inside base must not be flat but slightly curved, and the thinning and shaping movement is made outwards and upwards at
the same time and from the very first movement of shaping. If

Fig 32   Sections of a bowl showing the stages in throwing. Note how the inside shape develops

Fig 33   The two hands working together to shape a bowl. Left hand controlling edge, and right thumb and forefinger squeezing and lifting the clay to form the third stage in fig. 32

this is not done, the bowl either becomes too tall and will collapse when the edges are extended too far and become thin; or, if too open to begin with, it will collapse with the weight of the unthinned clay and the outward thrust of the wheel. The outer edge is always kept rather more vertical than desired till the very last movement of shaping, for the reasons mentioned above.

When making bowls, many people find that the most difficult part is to give adequate outside support to the lower portion of the bowl when thinning the walls; but this is important because otherwise you will fail to keep a continuous curve for the inside shape (fig. 38). Again, it is the internal shape that should decide the external profile, though this will also depend on how well the necessary turning will be executed (page 40).

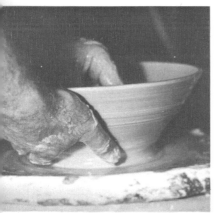

Fig 34   External view of fig. 35 showing outside support to bowl

Fig 35   Completing shaping of a bowl with right hand supporting the outside, and sponge pressing gently against the right thumb and together shaping the inside

Fig 36   Shaping and thinning a bowl with fingers and giving correct external support to base of bowl. For larger bowls, knuckling is necessary but the same precautions and principles apply

Fig 37   Continuing to shape small bowl with tips of fingers

Fig 38   What happens when external support at base of bowl has been inadequate

It is only in the intitial stage of throwing a bowl that the knuckles are used, as greater delicacy of pressure is needed with the fingers when the clay is moving and being aided by the out-ward thrust of the moving wheel. When shaping a large bowl it is often a help to support the outer profile with the whole palm of the right hand, while shaping or thinning with the left fingers or a small sponge held in the left hand (figs 34 and 35).

The shallower the bowl, the wider the initial centered clay needs to be, and when ready it will consequently need more turning than a deep bowl. When opening out a large shallow bowl, more control is gained by pressing with the fleshy outer palm of the right hand (fig. 39). The same technique is best used when opening out a dish which has a flat base but vertical or sloping sides, such as fig. 40.

Fig 39   Using fleshy part of outer palm to flatten and smooth clay prior to making
a plate or dish as in fig. 40. Again left hand controls edge. Note how both
hands work firmly together

Fig 40   Cross section of dish showing shape and distribution of thickness

Fig 41   Grooving flattened clay on wheel-head to take bat

Fig 42   Placing dampened bat on wheel-head. If the bat is too dry, it does not adhere well

Dishes are best thrown on bats (below) in order to help the base to dry, and so that they do not distort (which is almost impossible to prevent with large pieces) if removed from a wheel-head by hand as described earlier. For both dishes and bowls, the final shaping needs extremely light pressure with the tips of the fingers, and should be done with confidence and without hesitation, and with the minimum of movements.

Bats

The use of bats for throwing is common where certain shapes are too big or too difficult to lift or slide off the wheel-head. They can be made of either wood, plaster or asbestos, and should be circular in plan. In order to fix them to the wheel-head first centre a small ball of clay, then flatten it till it forms a half-inch layer on the wheel-head. With the tips of the fingers, as in fig. 41, make grooves in the surface, and then press the bat firmly in position in the centre of the wheel-head (fig. 42). It will be held partly by the moistness of the clay and partly by the suction of the air in the grooves. Before applying the next bat, sprinkle some water on the clay to moisten it in order to assist the adhesion, and lightly damp the bat.

A bat also helps to dry the base of the pot in preparation for any necessary turning.

Bats are used in a workshop for throwing plates, wide dishes and sometimes large pots which cannot be lifted from the wheel without assistance. Plates are made in the same way as dishes, but comparatively little clay is needed to form the edge (figs 39 and 43).

Fig 43   Using edge of thumb to level inside surface of plate, with right hand adding
          firmness

Large Shapes

Beginners should not immediately start by making large shapes,
but if you have the physique and confidence by all means practise
them. In broad principle, for large shapes you use the whole of
your hands for centering and opening up, rather than using
knuckles and fingers.

Opening up is often done with the outer fleshy part of the
right hand as in fig. 44, and the initial lifting of the clay into a
thick cylinder by using the palm of the left hand as when centering
(figs 45 and 46). The shaping is done with knuckles and fingers,

Fig 44   Opening out large bowl with outer palm of right hand working together
          with left hand

Fig 45   Method of lifting and squeezing up clay for cylinder of large shape

Fig 46   Another view of the operation shown in fig. 45. Note firm direct pressure with palm of left hand

and for large shapes it may be necessary to stand on a low platform to gain sufficient height to work easily.

It is usually the size of the kiln that restricts the making of large shapes, but really big shapes can be made either in several pieces and then joined, or by throwing a big base and lower sides, and, when firm enough, adding thick coils which are then thrown to extend the walls. This is repeated until the shape is finished. Allowance must be made for the continuing shrinkage of the lower half. Fig. 47 shows a large shape made in more than one piece and joined. It also has added thrown shapes.

Turning

Turning is the trimming of any excess thickness of clay with a sharp tool, with the pot spinning comparatively fast.

Fig 47   Student working on large shape made from thrown sections joined and added

The ideal of all good throwing is to make the maximum use of a given quantity of clay in the forming of a shape, and to throw so that the minimum amount of turning is needed.

As mentioned earlier, the inside shape determines the form, and any turning confirms this form and gives an even thickness to the walls of the article. When making a hollow-stemmed shape (fig. 48) it may be necessary to turn away quite a lot of clay, as a greater thickness is left at the base when throwing, to support the heavier upper part of the pot until ready for turning.

For most people the article to be turned needs to be held firmly in a chuck, or directly onto the wheel-head with soft clay. I have seen highly skilled turners holding the article centred on the wheel with only the downward pressure of one finger or thumb, turning the article with the other hand. This, however, is more easily done with bowls which have a low centre of gravity. For most of us a firmer hold on the pot is necessary.

Fig 48   Hollow stemmed vase where base needs to be fairly thick and where turning will be necessary

Fig 49   Placing pot to be turned in metal chuck, with added turned clay edge to take shape of pot

Fig 50   Placing pot in leather-hard clay chuck fixed to the wheel-head as shown in fig. 53

Fig 51   Turning tool held at angle to pot when turning to avoid juddering (wobbling) or corrugations in clay. Note how the base has been levelled first and then the sides turned, before the foot-ring is determined

Fig 52   Turned pot showing relatively even thickness of walls, base and foot-ring for even drying and satisfactory firing

Chucks can be of two types. You can either turn a coil of plastic clay on the edge of a metal chuck (fig. 49) and then insert the article to be turned; or you can have a selection of leather-hard thrown clay chucks (fig. 50) which can be fixed on the wheel-head, and which can be stored for long periods when not in use by wrapping in polythene (polyethylene).

Most professional throwers turn their pots (if this is necessary) immediately after throwing, cut them off the wheel-head with a twisted wire, and do nothing further. For those less skilled, turning in the leather-hard state is generally necessary.

Once the pot is firmly held in the chuck, the turning should be carried out with the wheel running as fast as is practical. The turning tool should never be held parallel to the wall of the pot but at a slight angle, to avoid juddering (wobbling) or corrugations in the surface of the clay (fig. 51). The base should be levelled first, then the sides trimmed, and finally the foot-ring shaped. Whatever the shape of the pot, the aim is to have as much of it as possible consistent in thickness (fig. 52). This helps it to dry evenly, and reduces the chances of cracking.

Fig 53   Effective but simple method of fixing chuck or large pot to wheel-head in order to turn any necessary clay from lower half of pot. The best way to turn tall thin shapes

A very tall shape may first be turned by damping the flat base and fixing it on the wheel-head as when thrown, centering the pot, then pressing with a knife point just above the wheel-head to force the clay downwards and bind it to the wheel-head (fig. 53). It can then be inverted and held with plastic clay as in fig. 54, to turn the base and foot ring. It is often helpful to place it over a solid, stiff clay cylinder, turned to the exact internal diameter of the neck of the pot.

Fig 54   Fixing an oval pot to wheel-head with thick coil of plastic clay.

Fig 55 Drawing showing different methods of
turning bowls
  (a) resting rim of bowl on the surface of a
      slightly moist, thin layer of soft clay spread
      or turned on the wheel-head
  (b) holding rim of bowl on the wheel-head
      with a coil of clay
  (c) supporting bowl on a dome of damp clay
  (d) supporting large bowl on clay which has
      been attached to a jar fixed to the wheel-
      head, for turning when bowl is larger than
      tray of wheel

Bowls or plates may be turned in several ways, as shown in fig. 55.

When turning a bowl you should think of the foot-ring as a ring of clay attached to the surface of a dome, with the shape of the dome being a continuous curve. If very large bowls are wider than the throwing tray, they may be inverted and rested on some article that has been fixed onto the wheel-head, as shown in fig. 55 d.

It is often difficult for the beginner to calculate the thickness of a large bowl's base, and it is undesirable to keep removing it while turning, to feel the thickness. A simple method of solving this problem is to take a thin piece of matchstick, equal in length to the required thickness of the turned base, and press it into the inside base of the bowl. You can then turn the base until you strike the wood splinter, and the splinter may be removed and the small hole filled with soft clay.

Cups are best turned on a cone of plastic clay (fig. 56).

Fig 56   Cup placed on a clay dome for turning

5   Developing the technique

Constant practice, and finding out how to overcome particular problems, is the only way of achieving proficiency as a thrower, Once you have gained confidence in making simple shapes, you can plan a series of exercises or tasks that will increase your knowledge and experience and improve your standards.

Throwing should be a rhythmic operation, and you should aim to reduce the number of movements in making a pot to the absolute minimum, finish it, and be on to the next one.

As a first exercise, take at least twelve balls of clay of equal weight, and throw a simple shaped bowl or beaker of the same size with each piece. The desired accuracy or perfection will come with practice, so do not worry unduly about these qualities to begin with. Throw one set as fast as possible and another slower, and compare the results.

As a change and contrast, take another dozen balls of clay of varying size and weight, and make different shapes, making some as thin as possible and varying the shapes as widely as you can from one piece to the next. Discipline must be balanced by freedom, but many people fail by not achieving sufficient initial discipline of technique. This must eventually become an unconscious act if you are to be a good thrower. Throwing is essentially a skilled technique which may be combined with a personal or individual feeling for form.

Other exercises could be to make a shape as tall or as narrow as possible with any given quantity of clay, or, again with a given quantity, to make as round a shape as possible and finish it with the narrowest possible neck. You will soon discover which are the most difficult shapes to throw, and these will be the ones to concentrate on, so set yourself exercises based on these and go on practising them.

When practising, it is often a help to cut the pot in half vertically with a wire or nylon thread, to check how even the walls and base are, before starting the next one. In this way you are constantly aware of your progress and will not go blindly on repeating mistakes. Some idea of what the pot should look like when cut is shown in figs 17, 30 and 52.

Stack throwing

Instead of throwing each article from a fresh lump of clay, the best and quickest method of making small bowls, cups, lids and spouts is by stack throwing. This is done by centering a large lump of clay and throwing the article from the top of it, and then

Fig 57   Stack throwing bowls from a large lump of clay

Fig 58   Cutting the bowl off with steel needle inserted into a piece of wood for a handle. This movement is done without stopping the wheel

cutting it off with a wire or a long needle (often without stopping the wheel or reducing speed) before throwing the next one (figs 57 and 58).

Jugs, mugs, cups and saucers

Whether you are throwing for profit or pleasure, you will at some time wish to make jugs, mugs, or cups and saucers. Although these may appear to be simple, straightforward objects, it is surprising how few one finds that are really successful. This is nearly always due to the fact that human nature tends to ignore the obvious and simple basic facts.

For a jug the basic essentials are as follows:
a.   It must be stable when full and being carried on a tray.
b.   The handle must be firm, comfortable and easy to grip, and not too big and coarse for small hands.
c.   The contents should flow gradually and easily, and not come in a sudden rush, either immediately or after continuous tilting.

47

d. The handle should be so placed that no strain is experienced when lifting a full jug or when pouring.
e. A jug should not be unreasonably heavy when empty.

Now for mugs, cups and saucers:

a. Cups are time and again quite unstable, with too small a base, but this is less often a failing with mugs.
b. Handles of mugs and cups are seldom really comfortable, are often too small, and occasionally too large.
c. Many mugs are uncomfortable to drink from, with too narrow a top and sometimes too thick and coarse an edge.
d. The form of both cups and mugs should be very simple, as they are in constant use and are regularly washed and dried.
e. As with jugs, the unfilled weight is even more important, as the fingers will feel the strain rather than the arms.

It is a good idea to study closely some of our traditional wares to find out just why they were made as they were. In the days when a country potter made useful articles for his public they had to function, and function well, or his business declined.

Making cups and saucers

Making a cup is very similar to making a bowl, but a cup is generally deeper and smaller. The most difficult part is to make the base sufficiently wide and stable without the shape becoming squat and dull.

The saucer, according to size, is made by centering into a low dome of clay and opening out as for a plate, or similar to when making a bowl. Saucers are best made on bats (see page 38) to avoid distortion before turning.

The main points to be considered with a cup and saucer are:

a. The saucer must be big enough for the cup, and easily picked up from a table or tray, so there must be sufficient rise in the shape of the outer edge to allow fingers to slide comfortably underneath.
b. The cup should fit easily and with stability in the well of the saucer.
c. The teaspoon should remain immobile on the shoulder of the well and not slide down when the cup is lifted from the saucer. This is not helped if the edge of the saucer is too high.
d. Saucers must have a wide stable foot-ring.
e. Cup handles should be high enough for the fingers to comfortably clear the edge of the saucer when lifting the cup, and without first having to tilt the cup.

48

f. Above all, the cup handle must be sufficiently robust for constant use, and a pleasure to grip.

Making jugs

Jugs tend to fall into two categories, those with a full or flowing outline, and those with a more severe, cylindrical shape. In traditional ware, the fuller shaped jugs tended to have a smallish neck and high handle for a very good reason—that they were used as carriers of liquid, did not easily spill when in motion, and could hang comfortably when carried long distances in the fields at harvest time.

The severer type was used more at table and in the home, and worked on the principle of having a small lip or spout. These poured easily but because of the jug's shape the flow of liquid was abruptly cut off when pouring ceased.

Spouts, knobs, handles and lids

From single forms you can proceed to the more difficult additions of spouts, knobs, handles and lids.

SPOUTS

Spouts that are formed from the jug itself should be generous or crisp according to the form of the jug, but not so small that the liquid flows over the extreme edges of the spout. A flow of liquid is preferable to a dribble. If the neck of the jug flares outwards sufficiently, the spout can easily be shaped as demonstrated in fig. 60. If the neck is straight, the tips of the fingers support the neck and are held in the same position as in fig. 60; the first finger of the other hand works from side to side to stretch the clay slightly, and is then drawn gently outwards to give curve or flow to the lip, while all the time the thumb and forefinger continue to support the neck.

Closed spouts (as for teapots) are thrown separately, and most people find it difficult to make them tall enough. They should be thrown in the same way as a cylinder, but the walls must start to slope inwards from the beginning (see figs 59 and 61 a–h). When the spout is leather-hard, cut it as shown in fig. 61h with a sharp knife, to fit the curve of the pot. Hold the spout against the pot and draw a thin line round the base of the spout with a sharp tool. Remove the spout and make a series of holes in the pot,

Fig 59   Shaping a teapot spout using the tips of the fingers (see also fig. 61)

Fig 60   Shaping half of a thrown shape to be used as an open spout for a coffee pot

inside the marked space, with a round metal or wooden tool of about $\frac{3}{16}$ in. diameter, and then attach the spout as described below.

Open spouts are made from thrown shapes as in fig. 60, and then cut off along the line indicated, to fit the pot. After attaching the spout, cut away the section of the pot behind it, either completely or leaving a bridge of clay to form a continuous rim.

Fig 61   Sectional drawings of a spout, showing throwing progression. After throwing, the spout is cut off as indicated

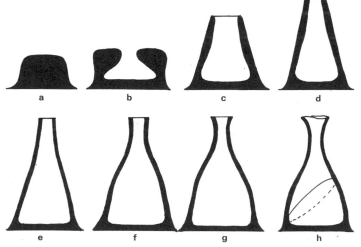

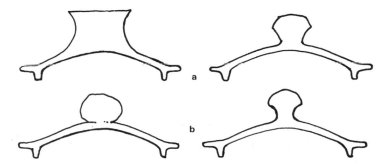

Fig 62   (a)   Lid before and after turning the knob
            (b)   Turned lid with knob thrown from small ball of clay

Spouts, like handles (see below), are best attached by wetting the areas to be joined with the finger and rubbing till a film of slip is formed, and then joining the two areas together. In this way they are less likely to crack off than when attached with too liberal an application of prepared slip, which will shrink when drying and leave a crack or space between the body and the spout.

KNOBS

Knobs may be turned from the surplus clay left for the purpose on the lid, as shown in fig. 62a. An alternative method is to trim off all the surplus clay, making a dome, and then throw a knob from a small ball of clay, using very little water (fig. 62b).

HANDLES

Handles are an essential part of many domestic shapes (see fig. 63).

Jug handles naturally vary according to the size of the jug. For the largest, the whole hand is needed to grip the handle and lift the jug. For medium jugs two or three fingers can comfortably be used, and for small jugs one or two fingers are sufficient.

Whatever the size of the jug, the handle should be comfortable and appropriate.

The simplest method of deciding the most comfortable grip for a handle is to roll a coil of fairly stiff clay and fold it loosely round the palm of the right hand, making a shape similar to a jug handle. Lay it on the bench for reference, as shown for the pulled handle in fig. 69. Then use this rough model as a basis for making pulled handles for jugs. Use the same method for designing one- or two finger handles.

This also applies to cups and mugs, but in this case it is very much the fingers that grip, rather than the whole hand. For attaching all forms of handles (including those pulled on the pot, page 55), it is best to wet the area of the pot where the handle is to be fixed and work up a film of slip from the clay surface, as described for spouts.

The cross-sectional form or shape of handles is most important. Both for strength and comfort, a basically oval shape is the most satisfactory. Round handles tend to move or slip when gripped, and over-flat, strip-type handles lack strength and, if at all wide, are uncomfortable and difficult to grip and will break easily if knocked.

Fig 63   The handle of the casserole on the right is hollow; it has been thrown and then joined in the leather-hard state.

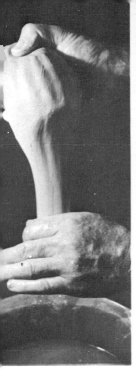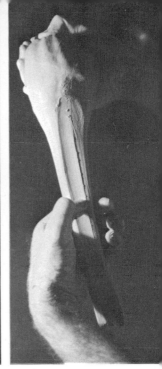

Fig 64   Pulling handle from lump of clay. Notice squeezing movement from right side of clay

Fig 65   Completing movement of squeezing from left side of clay to ensure symmetrical section to handle

Fig 66   Cradling handle in crook of little finger and shaping with end of thumb

Thrown handles are generally made solid, but larger ones need to be hollow. These are made in much the same way as a teapot spout (page 50) but are closed at one end.

Pulled handles can be made from one end of a large lump of clay as shown in figs 64–6. As each one is finished, it is pinched off with the fingers, and then another is pulled. The pulling and squeezing motion should be firm, gentle and rapid, never slow or jerky. When finished, the handles should be placed in rows upon a board and allowed to dry to a firm but plastic state. Then fix the upper end to the pot and, in one movement, bend to form the desired shape and fix at the lower end; or shape the handles first, as in fig. 69. Handles that are over-worked lose their spring and become lifeless.

Fig 67   Romano-British pot showing vitality and spontaneity of throwing

Fig 68   Thrown shapes by Hans Coper showing masterly control of form and texture

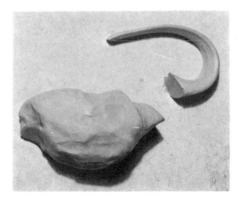

Fig 69   Handle pulled from lump of clay, cut off, and placed on board to dry ready for application

The most lively handles are those pulled directly on the pot (figs 70–73). To do this, start by pulling a long cylindrical coil, thicker than you want the finished handle. From this, break off a length of clay, and, after wetting the area of the pot where the handle is to be fixed, press the clay firmly onto the pot as in fig. 70, and carefully note the grip. The main pressure is with the second finger and ball of the thumb, with thumb and first finger acting mainly as guide. If possible, hold the pot with the handle hanging downwards when pulling, or keep vertical as in figs 70 and 71, and then shape and attach it as in figs 72 and 73.

LIDS
Lids can be thrown, according to size, from single lumps of clay, or by stack throwing as described on page 46 and shown in figs 74–6.

opposite

Fig 70   Pushing thick length of clay to adhere to pot ready for pulling

Fig 71   Pulling the handle on the pot. With this technique, handles are very unlikely ever to come off

Fig 72   Shaping the handle before attaching lower end

Fig 73   Clean crisp fixing of lower end of handle

Fig 74   Drawings showing the various stages of making lids by stack throwing

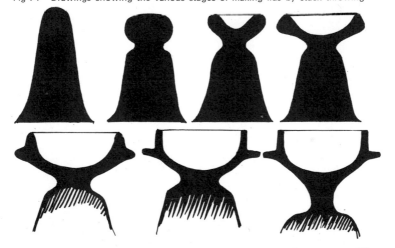

Fig 75   Shaping the flanges of a lid

Fig 76   Pinching off a finished lid from the lump when still in motion, but leaving
sufficient clay for turning the knob as shown in fig. 62

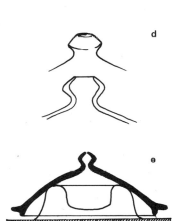

Fig 77 Method of making large lids
where the knob is thrown from
part of the lid when in a leather-
hard state
a Thrown lid on wheel-head. Note
hole in base of lid
b Lid still on wheel-head ready for
placing on bat, but with egg-cup
in position to retard drying of
area close to hole
c Lid in position ready to have
knob thrown
d Showing shape and section of
knob
e Finished lid with ventilation hole

For large lids, such as for bread bins, it is common to throw
from one lump of clay, make a hole in the centre of the base to the
wheel-head with the thumb or first finger, and then cut off and
place on a board to dry (fig. 77a). Place an egg-cup or small bowl
over the hole while drying to keep it damp (fig. 77b). When the
rest of the lid is firm, invert it over a dome-shaped chuck (fig. 77c).
Then insert the first finger of the left hand into the hole and use
the thick clay of the lid to throw and shape the knob, leaving a
hole in the middle for ventilation (figs 77 d and e).

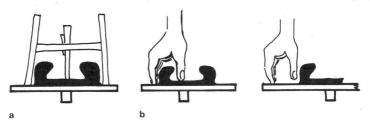

Fig 78   Two methods of checking thickness of clay at base of pots
(a)   Wooden adjustable tool
(b)   Approximating method, using thumb and hand

Faults in throwing and their correction

1.   Clay that will not centre. This happens quite often, due to the fact that, in coning and flattening the clay, it has been allowed to mushroom outwards and fold over, trapping a thin film of slip which fails to combine with the firmer clay. This leaves moist seams in the ball of clay, giving an uneven consistency.

2.   When throwing almost any shape, nearly all beginners fail to leave sufficient clay on the wheel-head to make a satisfactory base. There are two ways of checking that this does not occur. The first is a very old country technique of making a wooden tool, as shown in fig. 78a, that can be adjusted to show the required thickness. The other way is simply to hold the thumb and hand rigid as in fig. 78b, lift it out to one side of the pot, keeping it still stiffly vertical, and observe the distance between the end of the thumb and the spinning wheel-head. As a rough guide I have always found this satisfactory.

3.   A common fault is to have too narrow a base, and this comes from not paying sufficient attention to what one is doing inside the pot, because when finished the inside profile should determine the external shape.

4.   When lifting the clay (fig. 13, page 19) there is a common tendency to squeeze too firmly, and suddenly find that the top half has come away, and you have a thick collar of clay in your hand. Squeezing must be firm, but relaxed and not tense. Beginners tend to hold their breath throughout certain operations. Try to breathe normally.

5.   Pots with walls too thick near the base. This results from not being bold enough when first knuckling up the clay as in figs 15 and 16 (page 20). At first you will over-do it and twist, or pull the pot apart, but after practice on medium to small cylinders you will soon attain the correct balance of pressures. If the clay is not lifted and squeezed up initially, it is almost impossible to do it at a later stage. A well-thrown shape should need practically no turning at all at the base when finished.

6. Twisting or wrinkling of the clay in the cylinder stage, when throwing, is generally due to the need for over firm pressure because the clay is really too hard for throwing. It can also occur with clay in the correct state, if the surface, or fingers, have not been kept sufficiently wet or moist. On the other hand, it will also occur naturally if you have gone on throwing too long and the clay becomes paper thin and therefore weak. A pot that reaches the full thrown cylinder state with a long slow twist is generally suffering from badly wedged clay that has not expanded evenly under pressure.

7. Pots sometimes collapse and show vertical cracks as they subside. This is often due to using too much water in the initial stages of throwing, and failing to remove it with a sponge (or a sponge tied to the end of a stick). The water builds up and softens the inside walls, which suddenly fail to support the heavy top half of the pot, with the obvious results.

8. An undulating edge to the top of a pot. After every full movement in throwing, the top edge should be checked and made to run smoothly and level, as described in chapter 3 (figs 18 and 19).

9. A bowl with a bumpy inside profile. Fig. 38, page 36, shows a typical example. This is a very common fault, due to giving insufficient support to the lower outside of the bowl when thinning and shaping at the stage illustrated in fig. 36.

10. A correctly turned pot that no longer has the intended shape. This is the inevitable result of failing to visualise and create the shape in relation to the inside profile.

11. Saucers and plates that tip easily. Both of these articles need a wide base or foot-ring, especially plates. It is often wise to have both an outer and inner foot-ring for a plate. This aids stability and also supports the wide flat central area.

12. Knobs that are too small to handle, or bad for gripping. At first it is always best to make knobs bigger than necessary, till the correct size has been gauged as a result of practice. They should be so shaped that the fingers grip them easily, even when wet or when oven gloves are being worn.

13. Vases that are unstable. One does not make a shape and then arbitrarily decide to use it as a vase. The other half of the vase is the flowers, and you can't make a good vase without first taking the flowers into account. Failure to do this is proven by the great dearth of really practical and satisfactory flower vases. From a throwing point of view, a sufficiently wide and stable base is the prime consideration, to which must be related the shape of the vase, its appearance and usefulness.

Figs 79-90
Series of photos of a traditional Cornish thrower making the famous Cornish Pitcher, taken in early 1950's

Note guide stick for height of finished pot. Observe throughout how he throws with direct use of his body

Fig 80
Opening up with both thumbs

Fig 81
Forming inside base
with clenched
knuckles

Fig 82
Defining top of jug
before further thinning
of walls

Fig 83
Thinning the walls

Fig 84
Folding over and
thickening top edge
of pitcher

Fig 85
Shaping with
knuckles and fingers

Fig 86
Final shaping using
metal rib on outside to
give a smooth firm
surface to pot

Fig 87
Shaping spout

Fig 88
Using wooden
template under neck

Fig 89   Cutting pot off the wheel-head

Fig 90   Lifting pitcher with left hand and forearm and right hand

6 The grammar of shape

Your endeavour, once you have acquired the necessary standard of skill, will be to put it to practical use in making shapes and objects compatible with present day needs (see also chapter 7).

Most shapes in the past have been evolved for very specific practical reasons, either functional or purely decorative.

Whether thrown or hand-built, a piece of pottery can be said to be sculptural and three-dimensional. Thrown shapes are very like architecture in that they depend for their success on satisfactory proportions. This may possibly be rationalized, but it is something on which people with developed sensibilities can generally agree. Studies have been made on the relative proportions of pots in the same way as rules and laws of proportion have been worked out for painting and architecture.

Fig 91   A series of drawings showing how forms grow from the horizontal to the vertical

Fig 92   Large pot with applied decoration, made from thrown shapes joined in the leather-hard state

In chapter 4, I described the making of a range of shapes, and this range can be seen clearly in a series of forms growing from the flat waterlily-leaf shape of a coupé plate to the oval closed shape of the lily bud (fig. 91).

Within this initial range of forms there are endless variations that can be practised. A thrown shape may appear to be composed of more than one form, and is in fact often made of two or more separately made forms joined together (fig. 92).

One instinctively judges weight in relation to shape, and while the lightness of a large pot is often surprising, one should never be conscious of its being too heavy.

Most domestic ware is related in scale to the human being, and in particular to his hands and what they can easily and comfortably hold. Volume is also relative to one or a specific number of persons, and only in hand-made ware can truly individual wishes, needs, or tastes really be catered for.

The first essential of a shape is that it fulfils its function with ease and simplicity, and this was the basic philosophy of the Bauhaus. However, not only the shape, but also the material it is made of, and its treatment, should give pleasure to the user. This is where the ideas and personality of the potter can be equally expressed.

As we have seen, stability is often the determining factor with many shapes such as a water jug, cups and saucers that may be carried on trays, or a vase for a single flower that will be used on a restaurant table and is likely to be moved often. The shape of a neck or a spout should be carefully considered, and the design related to such practical problems as easy pouring and cleaning. In fact the very simplest shapes are the easiest to use and clean.

When a thrown shape is made for an unusual or specific function it then becomes a more exacting design problem.

With experience, one finds that something new and different in relation to form in functional ware is so often the result of the solution to a particular problem or need. It therefore has a reason —and, conversely, when a difference of shape is due to novelty alone, it often fails to be convincing or really relevant.

Functional domestic ware can therefore be viewed with some basic criteria before being assessed from a more aesthetic point of view. This is dealt with in detail in chapter 5, when discussing some of the necessary essentials of jugs, cups and saucers.

When dealing purely with sculptural qualities and ideas in clay, the potter's talents and aesthetic sensibilities must be of a high order, or the work will quickly suffer, and will join the vast sea of indifferent so-called ceramic sculpture that is so plentiful today in many countries. As most so-called ceramic sculpture is mainly hand-built, there is a limitation to what can be made by throwing.

As we said earlier, a thrown pot is essentially a free-standing sculptural form. It has a top and a bottom, or a beginning and an end. It also has a middle, which is equally important, and might be described as the line between two points, but this must be definite, and never hesitant. Its beginning, middle and end all fuse and integrate, to give an individual identity. No two thrown pots can ever be identical, just as no two thumb prints are absolutely the same.

The throwing of a pot is similar to any feat of skill, where the executant has full control and confidence in relation to every move he makes, and can tell you with assurance how successful any particular operation has proved.

A successful pot has a spring, a life of its own, a special magic, and gives an impression that it has just taken a deep breath, reached its maximum potential, and held it. Another quality it expresses is one of infinite economy of means, so evident in a Rodin drawing where sureness of line gives us something almost breathtaking.

Only in the actual experience of the act of throwing can you begin fully to understand the qualities I have been trying to describe.

Fig 93 American free thrown form with tachist-type decoration showing sympathy with modern painting

7 Ideas and how to execute them

Fig 94   Shapes for a vase or a teapot developed from the shape of an onion

Most of us are confident that we can recognize other people's ideas, but so often find it difficult to develop our own. If we base our ideas of shape on the work of other people we admire, or who are acknowledged as outstanding, at least we may be imitating the best. However, to develop a more personal approach to form we should be stimulated by the results of our own direct visual experience. This may vary in subject matter from the form of a tree trunk to the shape of an onion. Each may have qualities of form that attract us visually and which, by development and practice, we can translate and in some way express in a thrown pot. In this way our shapes will be much more our own, and should therefore express a personal conviction.

Ideas may be retained in the visual memory till you are actually in the act of throwing, or you can make a quick pencil outline for reference till ready to throw. Another good idea is to take a small piece of clay and roll or shape it in miniature to an approximation of the idea you wish to develop before beginning to throw.

There is much to be said for the practice of coiling before throwing. By this method a form is constructed slowly and methodically and its growth is more easily controlled. At the same time you will develop a sense of scale, as coiling should be generally used only for large shapes which, for beginners, would be too difficult to throw. The feel of plastic clay and how it behaves will then be familiar by the time you begin to use the wheel which, because of the speed at which you must work, leaves you little time to do more than try and control the clay.

Let us assume that you have been attracted by the shape of a large onion and feel that it has various possibilities that can be developed for ceramics. Two characteristics of the form could be the over-all shape, and the quality of curve that forms the shoulder. From the first might be developed a tall, oval vase, and from the second could grow an idea for a teapot (fig. 94.)

As there is nothing new under the sun, sooner or later you will see a shape made, say, 2,000 years B.C. that is almost identical to an idea you are working on. But at least you have the satisfaction of knowing that it was nevertheless your own idea. Almost any source of inspiration is legitimate but you should, however difficult, draw on your own experience rather than borrowing from others.

Once you have become involved with an idea, you should throw a whole series of shapes exploring its variations, and then choose two or three that are obviously the best and use these as your key shapes. For every new idea there will be a particular variation of throwing technique to be practised before you can easily express the particular quality of form or curve that attracted you. In this way you will consciously expand your vocabulary of technique as well as of shape.

A completely different approach can come from a need, rather than from a visual experience. For example, a thrown shape may be required to fulfil a particular purpose, and then the shape will be created to meet this requirement to the maximum satisfaction. Obviously the richer your vocabulary of form, the more stimulating the result will be visually, providing it also fulfils its function.

An excellent exercise for any potter is to develop a range of vases for some five or six types of flowers. The particular shape should show each type of flower to advantage, be stable when filled, particularly if subject to sudden draughts from open doors or windows, and hold sufficient water to need filling not more than once a day. Having fulfilled these main needs, the question of finish or colour for the surface of the vase will be equally important. Not all flowers are enhanced by being placed in a bright pink vase, nor does an over-decorated vase suit all types of flowers. These and many other questions of appearance, function and taste will need to be explored.

Gentle beating of a leather-hard thrown shape is almost as old as throwing itself. Care should be taken to suit the treatment to the shape, and again a series of experiments is the only way to find out what can be done.

The best method is to cradle the pot in one hand and begin by gently beating the cylinder along its length, or height, with a flat piece of wood about four inches wide. This is repeated on four sides until the cylinder is more square than round. The pot is usually turned first, and if it is slightly too dry for beating it can be quickly dipped in water once or twice and allowed to stand till the water has softened the clay to a more plastic state. Very pleasing results can be achieved by beating a series of cylinders of different widths and heights in this way. They can then be decorated or left plain with the possible later application of a coloured glaze (see chapter 8).

More difficult is the subtle shaping or incising of pots immediately after throwing, a technique used with mastery by Picasso. This is done immediately the pot has been lifted off the wheel, or an hour or two later when the clay is still soft but the surface is starting to become matt and is no longer shiny with wet slip. The shaping can be done with the hands, as in modelling, or the surface can be incised with a wooden modelling tool or a stick. Care must be taken that the pot does not collapse in the process of being shaped. A favourite subject for Picasso was the shaping of very graceful but simple female figures from tall, oval pots with a long, thin neck.

The necks and tops of pots are extremely important, and often tend to be dull. Here you can make a conscious effort by starting with a simple shape such as an oval, or even a sphere, and seeing how many different satisfactory tops or necks you can throw on a series of such shapes. This will also make you more critically aware when looking at pots in museums, where you can see an infinite variety.

The only way to discover the best foot-ring for a bowl is to try several on identical shapes and then decide which is the most satisfactory.

Thrown and turned ware

While good throwing should have a lively directness, it is also the basis for a somewhat different type of pottery called thrown and turned ware. Here the articles are thrown slightly thicker than required and, when leather-hard, are carefully and precisely turned over the whole of the external profile. Often beading, or raised and incised lines, are turned in the clay; and techniques such as sprigging (relief patterns of clay made by pressing clay into incised hollows in plaster) are used to decorate the smooth

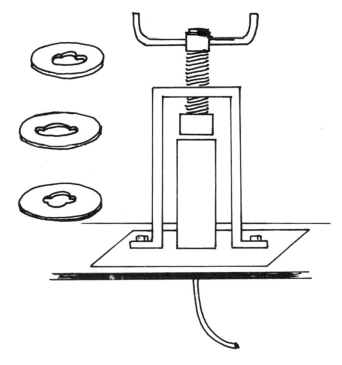

Fig 95   Dies and machine (commonly called a Dod box) for making strip handles
for thrown and turned ware

and precise surface of turned ware. If handles are applied, they
are made by extruding clay through a metal template from a Dod
box or extruder (fig. 95) and generally display decorative ribbing.
These strip handles are often plaited and twisted in order to
complement the precise and often severe forms. It was a technique widely used by the early industrial potters and has survived
in some factories until the present day. In recent years there has
been a revival and extension of the technique among young
potters who see it as a way of producing a type of individual
industrial product. Once they have mastered the various facets
of thrown and turned ware, there is considerable scope for the
imaginative treatment of form and decoration (fig. 102, page 80).

Fig 96   A series of traditional shapes

Cooking pots and kitchen ware

In recent years there has been a revival in the use of a whole range
of earthenware pots for baking, stewing, soup-making and other
forms of cooking, which are best made by throwing. Most of these
are imported from France, Spain, Portugal and Italy, where they
are still made in country potteries which are enjoying a consider-

Fig 97   An unusual cooking pot from Ghana, which is really a steamer. The steam
escapes from a hole in the saucer-like pieces, in which dishes of food are
placed to be cooked by the escaping steam

Fig 98   A selection of traditional cooking pots, as useful today as ever

able revival and patronage. Besides cooking pots, there are milk jugs, storage jars, wine carafes and very useful salt containers that all give plenty of scope for developing any potter's vocabulary of technique. Many of these shapes (fig. 96) have not changed for centuries, and are just as useful today as they have been for generations.

Because they are made of comparatively soft, porous earthenware, these cooking pots will withstand sudden and direct heat and can as easily be used on a gas flame as in the oven. Generally the clay used is an open red clay containing quite a lot of sand. The pots are often fired in the cooler part of the kiln, and the jugs, salt jars, wine carafes and mixing bowls in the hotter part to give a harder and more vitrified firing. Many of them are only glazed on the inside and occasionally partially dipped on the outside (see chapter 8).

There is practically no country that does not have some traditional cooking pot made of earthenware, and a very interesting study could be made of such pots and their uses. This would add both to one's gastronomic and one's ceramic experience.

Elizabeth David in London has recently opened a shop entirely devoted to selling a wide range of kitchen utensils and cooking equipment for household and professional cooking, which includes many articles made in earthenware and stoneware.

As most potters are good cooks, and the two have many terms and techniques in common, I show in fig. 98 a selection of cooking pots that are well worth trying to make and, at the same time, are a great pleasure to use.

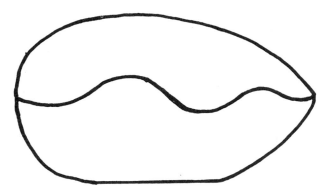

Fig 99   A romatoph for baking a chicken. Made of red terra-cotta clay and unglazed

It is an accepted culinary fact that food cooked in an enclosed container retains most of its goodness and flavour, so it is not surprising that once more a romatoph is becoming increasingly popular with people who appreciate the qualities of excellent cooking. Romatophs were and still are made from a red terra-cotta clay, thrown on the wheel and closed at the top when throwing, to form a shape rather like an egg, and then turned at the base when in a leather-hard state. They are then slightly flattened on one side, so that they stand firmly, and are cut into two pieces in a wavy line as shown in fig. 99, ensuring an accurate fit so that, when a chicken is being cooked, as little moisture as possible escapes. This vessel is unglazed and is most successful if soaked in water for some minutes before being filled and placed in the oven.

The Mediterranean countries are justly famous for their cooking and, not least among them, North Africa and the Arab countries. The Moroccans have a beautiful cone-shaped dish called a Touajen (fig. 100) which appears to work on the condensation principle, and is really a very crude form of pressure cooker. The food is cooked in its own juices which are given off in the form of steam, condensing on the inside of the cone and then running back into the aromatic mixture. Generally it is used for cooking joints of chicken with whole carrots, to which are added one or more cut lemons, together with the herb cumin, and then this basically sweet-and-sour dish is eaten with a type of semolina.

Another cooking utensil is the Mez-Mar or Kanoun, used for holding charcoal and cooking Kebabs, which may have been used

78

Fig 100   Moroccan Touajen for cooking. It is completely enclosed and works on
a crude pressure-cooker principle.

for centuries in African countries. Fig. 101 shows two common
types. The base is a support for the charcoal container and collects
the ashes and, at the same time, controls and protects the flow of
air to keep the charcoal burning. The grill or skewers holding the
meat are laid across the top edge above the glowing embers,
which naturally add flavour to the pork or lamb kebabs. Wood
and leather bellows are used to fan the charcoal when the heat
dies down.

Fig 101   Two types of Mez-mar or Kanoun—a North African utensil used for
supporting and holding a container of burning charcoal, over which
kebabs are cooked or grilled

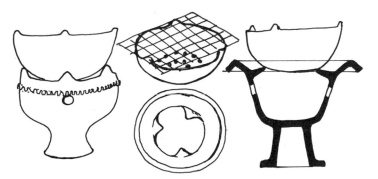

Fig 102   Pots showing the technique of throwing and turning as compared with free direct throwing

8 Firing, glazing and decorating

Biscuit firing

This is the name given to the first firing of a clay pot. In this firing, pots may touch each other and even be stacked one upon the other in the kiln, as long as they fit satisfactorily, and their weights are similar. In the same way, a series of various-sized bowls may be placed one inside the other, and this greatly reduces the cost of firing and makes the maximum use of space. A great deal of care is needed at the early stages of a biscuit firing as this is the most critical period. This is explained by the fact that two forms of water are present in clay, one called water of formation and the other chemically combined water. The first makes the clay malleable and plastic, and evaporates under normal drying conditions, and the thicker the clay the longer this evaporation will take. The chemically combined water is only expelled at a temperature between 450°C (842°F) and 600°C (1112°F) when the clay begins to change its chemical composition. The completion of this chemical change, when the firing is finished and the pots are cooled, gives the clay a hard, porous, biscuit quality.

Before this critical period, at about 200°C (392°F), the organic matter present in most clays begins to decompose and fire away. The chemical moisture comes away in the form of steam, and this must be a slow gradual process. If the firing is too fast at this stage, the steam builds up a pressure and the pot will shatter (which may give rise to the misconception that pots blow up in the kiln due to air bubbles in the clay). It is therefore imperative that plenty of ventilation is available at this stage to allow the steam to escape and be replaced by fresh air. Ventilation should continue to a lesser degree throughout the firing to clear the kiln atmosphere of the various fumes and gases that are produced in biscuit firing.

Once the critical period is past, the heat can be increased gradually and the firing can proceed steadily till the fusing or vitrifying stage is reached. This will vary with red earthenware clays from 900°C (1652°F) to 1100°C (2012°F), and up to 1140°C (2084°F) for some white earthenware bodies (see chapter 2). If you are uncertain about a clay's vitrifying temperature or it is not stated by the manufacturer, the only solution is to fire a pot first to about 1060°C (1940°F) and check its porosity. If it is fairly porous, refire to 1140°C (2084°F) and test again. At this stage you will generally find that the biscuit pot has a hard, slightly shiny surface and will absorb no water if damped. It will in all probability have shrunk considerably since the 1060°C

(1940°F) firing. From this test you would conclude that the clay's best biscuit firing temperature was between 1100°C (2012°F) and 1120°C (2048°F). The usual practice is to fire the biscuit ware slightly higher than the intended glaze firing, in order to overcome any warping, shrinking, or other defects, which will then be avoided in the glaze firing.

The temperature may be regulated by the use of a pyrometer, or with Seger cones that melt at set degrees of temperature and are placed so that they can be observed through the spy holes in the kiln door.

Biscuit ware when fired should still have a degree of porosity and this is easily tested by applying a wet tongue, or wetting the pot with a damp sponge, and seeing how quickly the moisture is absorbed.

When the firing is finished, and the kiln switched off, the ventilation holes should be closed so that no cold draughts pass through the kiln while cooling. These can cause cracking (or dunting) of pots towards the end of the cooling period and, as a general rule, it is best not to unpack until the inside of the kiln is bearably warm. The main point to remember when unloading a biscuit kiln, is to wipe off any sand that may have stuck to the pots that were bedded in it for support during firing. If this is not done at once it may be forgotten, and when the pots are later glazed over and re-fired, the sand will give a rough surface to the pot and glaze. The period of firing for biscuit is between nine and eleven hours, according to the type of ware and thickness of the articles. Very thin pots fire much more quickly than thicker ones.

Glazing

Glaze is a form of glass which is applied in its raw state to a biscuit pot and, when melted at specific temperatures, fuses to form a glassy, non-porous surface. Its appearance can vary very widely according to the basic ingredients from which it is mixed. For the beginner, however, it is possible to achieve a good variety of results from a limited range of glaze.

CHOOSING GLAZES

Manufacturers supply ready-prepared glazes to suit some of their clays, but, apart from clear glazes, they are seldom suitable for personal tastes. It is therefore far more satisfactory to choose a glaze with a wide fusing and melting range, that can be used first as a clear glaze. To this can be added various oxides to obtain coloured glazes, and an opacifier, such as tin oxide, for a white opaque glaze. An alternative method is to take one of the manufacturers' glaze fritts, which have a lower melting point than most glazes, and add between 10 per cent and 20 per cent of china clay to give a satisfactory glaze. With this method you can easily vary the melting point by varying the addition of china clay. By adding an excess of china clay, you will then have a matt glaze. In learning about glazes, it is a great help to take a set weight of fritt and start by adding 5 per cent of china clay. Repeat the test again with the same amount of fritt, adding another 5 per cent of china clay; and continue the test, each time adding a further 5 per cent. You will learn a great deal by observing the fired results. Make sure that they are all fired at the same temperature.

Once you have settled for a limited range of basic glazes, and they have all been well tested, make up some 5−10 lbs of each so that the glazes are always available when needed. Most earthenware, biscuit, and glaze firings will take place between 1040°C (1904°F) and 1120°C (2048°F), and within these limits your tested glazes will be quite satisfactory.

For making an opaque glaze, add between 8 per cent and 10 per cent of tin oxide. If cobalt is used for blues, as little as 0·5 per cent will give a very definite blue and 2 per cent, if applied thickly, gives a blue black. For copper, iron and manganese, you can use varying quantities from 1 to 6 per cent, and up to 10 per cent if a black glaze is required. Any combination of oxides should, if possible, not exceed a total of 10 per cent.

MIXING GLAZE
Apart from most of the oxides, the raw materials for making glazes are white in colour; so it is imperative that all materials are clearly labelled, and that you put out all your ingredients methodically, and, when any quantity has been taken from its container, immediately replace the lid.

The reason for glazes not performing as expected can often be traced later to errors in labelling, returning excess materials to the wrong containers, or forgetting to add one of the ingredients. Don't forget, too, that even manufacturers make mistakes, and sometimes send the wrong raw materials, possibly due to incorrect labelling. I have experienced this on more than one occasion and it has been quite costly in time and failure before the cause of the trouble was traced. Always list your ingredients and tick the list as each one is used or added to the batch. Use metric weights and then everything can be calculated easily in percentages.

When the glaze materials have been weighed into a bowl, add sufficient water to cover, and let it stand for an hour till the water has had time to soften the lumpy materials. Then stir to a thick liquid and sieve through a 100-mesh sieve with a stiff brush. Always mix glazes with water, never in the powder state, as the dust·from dry glazes can be injurious to health. Always start with the glaze too thick, as it can easily be thinned by adding more water. If it is too thin, you will have to wait for hours for the glaze to settle and then pour off the surplus water.

When you have made a glaze and sieved it, stir it extremely well so that the batch is consistent, and leave it to dry out. When almost dry, break up the mass and mix again before storing ready for use. If it has become too dry, then only mix by shaking the glaze in its container with the lid on.

APPLYING GLAZE

The thickness of the glaze to be applied will depend on the porosity of the biscuit ware, and only trial and error will teach you the correct thickness. Generally, a flowing, creamy quality is ideal. Glaze should only be watery for very soft biscuit, and thick for high-fired biscuit. Keep the glaze stirred all the time when in use.

To glaze the inside of a pot, pour in sufficient glaze to cover the area, and then pour it out slowly, revolving the pot at the same time to ensure that the whole of the interior is covered.

The outside may be glazed by pouring the glaze over the pot, or, if you have a sufficient quantity, by dipping the pot until the glaze comes almost level with the rim. Metal tongs are very useful for holding biscuit pots when they are being glazed by pouring and often when dipping. If you are lucky enough to have a spray gun and compressor, you can glaze the outside by spraying, but be extremely careful to use an adequate exhaust fan to take away the surplus glaze vapour, as this can be injurious to the lungs.

It is easier to glaze, handle and store biscuit fired pots, and in this state various forms of decoration are more easily applied. It is, however, possible to glaze pots in the raw and unfired state. This needs very skilled handling. The glaze used on raw pots must shrink to the same degree as the pot, in drying and firing, and must therefore contain a small amount of the same clay as the pot. Otherwise, the glaze can easily flake off as the pot dries. For this method, the glaze should be applied when the pot is leather-hard, or sometimes when bone dry. The glaze and biscuit firings are then combined in one operation.

Glaze firing

The main object in glazing earthenware is to counter the porosity of the ware, and make it waterproof. At the same time, the glaze gives a hard-wearing surface, which is also easily cleaned.

The pattern of a glaze firing is the opposite to that of a biscuit firing. Here the temperature may be increased fairly rapidly in the initial stages until 850°–950°C (1562°–1742°F) is reached. From this point, the rate of firing should be reduced, so that the glaze will have time to mature and react with the clay of the body. If you are firing to between 1060°C (1940°F) and 1080°C (1976°F), two to two-and-a-half hours should be allowed to complete the last 100°C (212°F). Glazed ware should never be fired for less than 8 hours, but need not take as long to fire as biscuit ware. If possible, the temperature may be kept at 1080°C (1976°F) for half to one hour, as this improves the quality of the glazes. This operation is called soaking. Great care must be taken in packing a glaze kiln because the powdery dry glaze is easily rubbed or chipped off the pots. By adding approximately one teaspoonful of water-soluble glue per gallon to the glaze, this hazard can be greatly reduced.

Glaze should be wiped off all foot-rings if the pots are to be placed directly on the kiln shelves. If not, they should be placed on stilts for support. A pad for cleaning the base of pots is made by tacking a piece of heavy felt across a 7–8 inch piece of thick board. If possible, strengthen the board to prevent warping when wet. The felt is then wetted under a running tap and the articles drawn across the felt. When the felt becomes too dirty, wash it under the tap.

Pots should never touch each other in a glaze firing, otherwise they will fuse together. At some time or other most of us have experienced this.

As with a biscuit firing, a degree of ventilation is necessary to keep a clean atmosphere in the kiln. Take great care in brushing the underside of kiln shelves before placing them in the kiln, so that no small particles of sand or other foreign matter will drop down onto the pots during firing and spoil the ware. Kiln shelves should have a three-point suspension with kiln supports under two adjacent corners, and the third in the middle of the opposite side. If more than one kiln shelf is used, the supports should always be placed in line vertically.

Glazed ware should be cooled in the same way as for biscuit firing. A cardinal rule is to clean the bottoms of all pots that have been stilted, immediately you remove them from the kiln. Small, sharp pieces of stilt adhere to the glaze where they touched the pot, and these pieces often need to be ground or knocked off. At the same time, draw the edge of a heavy file across the surface of the shelves as you unpack them to remove any sharp pieces of stilt that sometimes stick to them.

Decorating

OXIDES FOR DECORATING

All beginners are advised to start by using only the basic metal oxides of iron, manganese, copper, cobalt, antimoniate of lead for yellow, or a prepared yellow glaze stain. With these oxides, used either singly or in measured or calculated proportions, you will be able to produce an enormous variety of colours.

They can be used for various forms of decoration as described later in the chapter (page 87), or by being added to a clear glaze to make coloured glazes.

Iron Oxide gives a warm, pale brown to dark rust colour, according to strength, in decoration, and 6 per cent in a glaze will give a warm honey brown. It does not work well under an opaque or semi-opaque glaze, not fusing readily and easily with opaque glazes.

Manganese Oxide gives a pale mauve-black to pure black in decoration and 3 per cent—4 per cent in a glaze gives a half-tone mauve-grey. With 8 per cent—10 per cent in a glaze, the result is a deep purplish black.

Copper Oxide gives pale green to matt green-black when used as decoration. In glazes, 3 per cent—4 per cent gives a definite green and 10 per cent a matt, metallic black.

Cobalt Oxide is the most intense colour and, as already indicated, a very pale wash will give a positive blue when decorating. In a glaze 8 per cent or less, according to thickness of application, will give a deep blue-black.

Antimoniate of Lead or yellow stain should never be used too thickly as it does not melt so easily into a glaze as the other oxides.

While copper, cobalt, and manganese are black in their raw state, antimoniate of lead looks yellow and iron oxide has a deep rust-red colour. Other oxides can be used but, to begin with, the above offer ample scope for experiment.

BRUSH DECORATION

By using the basic oxides at various strengths they may be applied to the raw pot, fired to biscuit temperature, and then glazed in the usual way. They may also be brushed on to the glaze before the glaze firing. To paint on the biscuit and then glaze and fire, is not always satisfactory, because while glazing the pigment may be disturbed and it tends to flow during the firing. So either decorate on the raw clay, or on top of the unfired glaze.

Basic oxides can also be successfully applied as decoration with a sponge, and this was a favourite method of the early Delftware painters.

Oxides come in various grades with the more expensive being water-ground. While for brush decoration they need to be finely ground, the coarser oxides, if unground, can give a rich speckled effect when added to a transparent or semi-opaque glaze. If more than one oxide is used, this can be equally attractive, and will be better still if the proportions are not equal.

GLAZE AS DECORATION

A hand-thrown pot automatically has a decorative surface quality as a result of the throwing technique. This can easily be accentuated by glazing with a slightly soft white or a coloured glaze. The higher ridges produced in knuckling will thus tend to break through the glaze giving pleasant colour variation to the surface.

Another successful method of decorating with glaze is first to glaze the inside of a red pot, and then with either a white or black glaze, half dip the outside. This will give simple colour contrast. An extension of this technique is first to brush a wide band of an oxide round the middle of a red earthenware pot. After glazing the inside in the usual way, half dip the outside with a white opaque glaze. When fired the result will be a pot with a white top and neck, an area of colour where the glaze covers the pigment, below this a band of dark fused pigment, and then the red biscuit lower section of the pot.

Many Japanese potters use a glaze on glaze technique, but mainly for stoneware pottery. The idea is first to glaze the pot with a single neutral or coloured glaze, and then skilfully pour a contrasting coloured or textured glaze across areas of the pot already glazed (see fig. 103). Another method is to pour only one glaze on certain areas of a biscuit pot and then fire to full glaze temperature. In this way the glaze is used entirely decoratively, because it is not essential for stoneware pots to be fully glazed.

DECORATING DIRECT ONTO CLAY

Some of the most suitable forms of decoration for thrown ware are those applied to the pot in a leather-hard or bone dry state. While a pot is comparatively soft it can be freely combed with a metal or wooden tool, and later glazed with a semi-opaque or clear glaze. Alternatively, a contrasting coloured slip may either be trailed on from a slip trailer when the pot is leather-hard; or the slip can be freely brushed across the surface, but this must be done while the clay is damp, otherwise the slip will flake off when drying.

Equally, an impression with a wooden, metal or plaster tool or die may be pressed into the damp clay surface, or a piece of soft clay can be applied to the surface as in fig. 92, page 68.

Another method, known as pierced ware, consists of cutting or piercing shapes or holes in a thrown form in the leather-hard state. An excellent example is shown in fig. 106 (page 99). This is basically a decorative technique, but is useful for such articles as ceramic lamps or candle holders.

SGRAFFITO

This is a simple technique where the pot is first covered, by dipping or pouring, with a contrasting coloured slip, such as white or black on a red pot. When it has dried till the shine has disappeared, patterns or designs can be scratched through to the surface of the pot underneath.

RESIST DECORATION

Resist decoration, using slip or glaze, has been practised by many potters throughout history. Wet cloth, leaves or paper, may be placed on the leather-hard clay surface and a slip poured over them. When the slip is matt-dry, the paper or material is peeled off, leaving a shape that contrasts in colour with the poured slip. This is sometimes repeated again with another coloured slip, or combined with the next technique of wax resist.

Fig 103   Dish showing contrast of one glaze poured across another as a form of decoration

WAX RESIST

This is used more with glaze than slip. The resist is generally applied with a brush. It can be a mixture of melted paraffin and paraffin wax applied when hot, a mixture of bees-wax and candle wax also applied when hot, or a very suitable cold wax resist that is bought ready-prepared and can be diluted with water if it is too thick (see page 100 for supplier). To be effective, the more liquid the cold wax resist, the better. When the wax has dried, the glaze or slip is poured over it in the usual way, and the wax will burn away when the pot is fired.

More precise and detailed forms of decoration are generally only applied to smoothly thrown surfaces, such as one sees on a fine Chinese or Korean bowl which has been enhanced with delicate and subtle incised patterns.

9   Equipment and premises

Wheels

There is possibly something more direct in throwing on a kick wheel, where you have direct physical control of both the speed of the wheel and the clay. Kick wheels are cheaper than power wheels, but like tailor-made clothes they need adjusting to the user, so ideally they should be custom built.

Many people make their own kick wheels, and often very successfully, but generally speaking it is best to commission someone whose profession it is to construct such things, making your requirements crystal clear. Absolute rigidity in structure is the first essential of a kick wheel, but this is more easily obtainable with welded metal construction than with wood.

When it comes to a power wheel, a metal frame construction is necessary for absolute rigidity. The speed should range from 40–60 revolutions per minute to 120–160. When centering a large piece of clay the wheel should maintain a constant speed, no matter how heavy the clay or varied the pressure. This is one of the first essentials when testing a wheel that you may intend to purchase.

A good range of speeds, especially the lower ones, and constant speeds under variable throwing and centering pressures, are the most important requirements for a power wheel.

The physical method of control for varying the speeds is important, and should be comfortable and not greatly disturbing to one's throwing technique.

General precautions

Before buying any equipment or acquiring premises for a home or professional studio, check accessibility for equipment and materials, then make a thorough check of what electrical, gas, water, or other facilities are available or will be needed. Know the exact electrical requirements for your kiln, wheel or other tools. Check whether drains are adequate and will not quickly block with slip, or other sedimentary materials, and even plaster, if you should wash bowls in a sink after using plaster.

If the studio is not on a ground floor, make sure you can install your machinery easily, and check that the floor will withstand the weight. As long as an electric kiln is used there will be little difficulty with insurance, but with combustible fuel such as gas, oil etc. it can be difficult.

Using and storing clay

A rigid bench, preferably against a wall, or alternatively a slate or stone platform fixed to brick piers, is needed for wedging.

Prepared clay should be wrapped in polythene (polyethylene) sheets or bags and stored in a metal or plastic bin till wanted. Dry clay should be soaked in water in a bowl, partially dried out on a slab of plaster, or air dried, preferably in a draught, till in a satisfactory state for wedging. Polythene (polyethylene) bags of all sizes are now available, and these can be placed over pots of almost any size, that need to be kept damp or in a leather-hard state for later turning. This avoids the necessity for a damp cupboard which can be expensive, if it is to be effective. It is essential to have suitable shelving for dry unfired and fired pots, and for this a rigid metal or wood construction is best, but of a type easily assembled, dismantled or moved.

Kilns

A kiln for beginners need not be large. The safest and easiest, for control and operation, is an electric kiln. The internal dimension need not exceed 15 ins wide × 15 ins deep × 16 ins high, and unless considerable quantities of wares are envisaged, this size is ample. Have it wired for high temperature firing, even if you may never fire to stoneware.

Where possible, a kiln should be in a well-ventilated room separate from the work space, as during firing noxious fumes are given off (particularly in the biscuit firing) and these can be injurious to health. Kiln makers will make frames in two halves for ease of access if this is a problem.

If, however, you live in a remote area with no electricity easily available, it will be a case of a kick wheel, and some form of natural fuel firing such as wood, oil or coal. There are many plans available for such kilns, and you can write to any craft pottery magazine, who will give you the necessary information.

Gas is a very satisfactory form of firing, but needs more skill and care than electricity.

Many potters today are turning to oil firing, and building their own kilns, some large and some quite small, so that they are not dependent on electricity or gas supplies which could suddenly be affected by power cuts or greatly reduced pressure. Generally crude oil is cheaper for firing than other fuels, but even this is subject to sudden changes and increases.

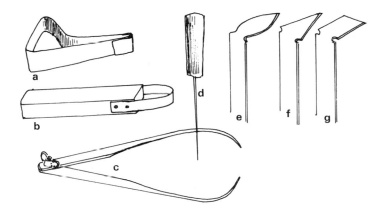

Fig 104   Selection of turning tools and other aids to throwing
     (a)   Turning tool made by bending a firm strip of packing case metal
     (b)   Wooden-handled tool with metal cutting edge (the shape of the
            metal can vary)
     (c)   Aluminium callipers for measuring the diameter of pots
     (d)   Large needle in wooden handle for cutting clay while throwing
     (e, f, g)   Three basic shapes for metal turning tools

Turning tools

Turning tools are a very necessary part of a thrower's equipment
and of course will vary with personal choice. Some people prefer
to make their own tools and this can be done by heating, bending
and grinding a strip of mild steel or even files. Tools used in other
professions can often be adapted for potting and many potters
turn their pots with a strip of shaped packing case metal. It can
be held comfortably and firmly in the hand, and is easily sharpened.
The essential requirements are a straight-edged turning tool and
one with a curved edge. To these may be added several variations
according to taste and the job·in hand (fig. 104).

     Most potters' suppliers will supply an adequate selection for
any beginner.

     Many dental and medical tools or instruments can suitably be
used in pottery. Even though files so easily get wet and rust, it
is still advisable to use one regularly for sharpening turning tools,
otherwise turning becomes a difficult and unattractive task.
Sharp tools are always a pleasure to work with in any profession
or craft.

Second hand equipment

You may be tempted, when beginning, to purchase a second-hand wheel or kiln. If it is a kiln, remember that while the kiln itself may be cheap, the cost of moving, installing and replacing elements that may soon wear out, could be more expensive than a new one. Only if it is practically new is it worth considering.

Second-hand wheels are often a better buy as long as you first check that possible worn parts would be easily replaceable. So often it may be an individually built wheel with no part that is standard. There is always some risk and possible expense in buying second-hand equipment, but if you do, always seek good professional advice first.

List of requirements

I would suggest the following as a minimum list of equipment and materials for anyone starting to throw for profit or pleasure:—

A small kiln of 2–3 kilowatts. Approx. internal dimensions 15 ins wide × 15 ins deep × 16 ins high

A satisfactory kick or power wheel

Approx. 4 hundredweight of red prepared clay ready for throwing

Two good natural sponges and one attached to a stick for getting water out of pots when they are finished

Plenty of twisted wire or some nylon thread

A good selection of turning tools

Plaster or asbestos bats

Some large sheets of light polythene (polyethylene). The kind used on building sites is too heavy

A deep metal chuck for turning, with diameter across top of 7–8 ins

One hundredweight of silver sand for mixing with clay, or using in kiln to bed in certain articles during biscuit firing

Sufficient kiln shelves and spares, plus props and stilts for glaze firing

A container for clay

Small containers for glaze, one 30–40 mesh sieve for coarse sand etc.

One 80-mesh sieve for slip

One 100-mesh sieve for glaze. It is worth having spares of these. They should all have phosphor-bronze mesh

Half a hundredweight of a good clear basic glaze to which can be added colouring pigments or an opacifier

A pyrometer or Seger cones for temperature control

Do not fail to check all materials immediately on arrival to see if you have received what you ordered or to check that it is in good condition and is the correct type. If you do not, manufacturers are less likely to be co-operative about replacements or exchanges.

Fig 105   Two thrown pots by Lucie Rie, which have been shaped in the leather-hard state. The left-hand one has sgraffito through glaze decoration, and the right-hand one shows an interesting use of textured glaze

10 Purpose and profession

Whether you learn to throw for personal pleasure or professional need, a worthwhile standard is the first essential. The basic practical difference is one of economics.

While the time for scholarship has to be financed, it is nevertheless difficult to calculate or relate accurately a financial return for such time. However, within our modern commercial system it is essential that we calculate a profitable monetary return on time spent (particularly in craft-based professions or industries), otherwise a financial loss ensues. Therefore a professional thrower must work to different criteria to one who throws for personal reasons alone, or with an attitude mainly of scholarship.

Let us look first at the professional thrower. To be successful he must not be limited in what he can throw, and he must be fast enough in his throwing to achieve the minimum quantity of production to make his position economically viable, as well as that of the rest of his fellow workers. A good thrower is often able to produce sufficient ware to keep between four and six other workers busy with such activities as preparing clay, attaching handles and spouts etc. where necessary, packing and firing kilns, glazing ware and performing all the other jobs connected with the finished article. He may therefore become, and often is, the key figure in a large workshop, and often behaves like a prima donna. This can be one of the weaknesses in a modern workshop, where machinery is more easily replaced than skilled human labour. Many small businesses have faltered and failed when a good thrower has decided to leave at short notice with no equivalent replacement available.

There is no doubt that, for a craftsman, his capital is his degree of skill, and this has often been used effectively as a bargaining instrument.

With today's increasing standards of living, it is very difficult (but still possible) to run single-handed a workshop based on thrown domestic ware. To survive, the division of labour as a team is a more satisfactory solution, and here goodwill and co-operation are very important. The price of the products must be reasonably competitive, but they must have sufficient individuality or style not to be comparable to an industrial product.

In commercial throwing, time is a deciding factor in both production and cost, and a thrower may prefer to be paid by piece-work rather than by the hour. It therefore follows that, if too much time is spent on each article at any given stage, (and particularly when throwing), it will greatly affect the finished cost. For this reason, in a commercial workshop, apart from the necessary application of handles or spouts, many articles are finished (as far as making is concerned) when the potter lifts them off the wheel. It can take as long to turn an article as to throw it, so for some workshops turning is reduced to an absolute minimum, and often used only for lids.

In workshops where turning is felt to be essential to the look and quality of the finished ware, you may find that this added cost is balanced by the sale and production of less standard but more individual wares which can command a relatively higher price for the time and costs involved. No one will dispute this as long as the business is economically viable.

This is also an essential pattern for those who run a workshop single handed. It is necessary to produce a steady flow of new ideas as well as a range of routine articles, in order to ensure survival.

To keep a balance between time spent on the minimum production necessary and time spent on developing new ideas is extremely difficult. The time spent on development or experiment has to be paid for, and in some way this cost must be included in the price of finished articles. Those who view their work professionally, even if only as a part-time occupation, must not fail to be realistic in their costing methods. Throwing therefore can be a full-time activity as part of a team, or a part-time activity as one phase of a wider operation all controlled by one person.

Other people may use throwing to develop shapes or ideas that will later be translated into designs for industrial production. They will then give due consideration to the industrial production techniques involved, but will never endeavour to reproduce hand thrown ware industrially.

Now let us look at the thrower from whom continuous production is not demanded. He may have more time to explore and develop the particular qualities of certain clay bodies in relation to specific ideas about shapes. He could do this as an artist potter, or in the capacity of a teacher of throwing. The results will tend to be more personal than utilitarian, but this so often acts as a stimulus and revitalizing influence to the production side of pottery.

For the artist potter, throwing is more a means of expressing certain ideas than a production technique. This becomes more obvious when technology is increasingly able to supply our domestic needs and we see ceramics moving closer to fine art as a means of expression.

As technology expands and increases throughout the world, there follows inevitable social and economic change. These changes in turn affect people's activities, and we find in so many fields that only two extremes operate. We find a world of dualities. With increasing technology there comes a great demand for designers to solve design problems, and on the other hand an increasing desire, and need for, the individual and unique object that expresses individuality and identity, rather than anonimity.

While pottery workshops employing several people still exist, it becomes increasingly difficult to keep this middle of the road balance which may soon become uneconomic. What happens is that the big merge and get bigger, and the small must become highly specialized or highly individual or cease to operate. In some cases the large firms see and fully appreciate the value of the small creative units, and intelligently incorporate them as part of the large whole. They then become, as it were, a small research team of innovators, exploring and developing ideas relative to materials and techniques.

Wherever one may come in all this, the ability to throw pots well or creatively is a very vital ingredient. In fact one may even be asked to write a book about it!

Fig 106   Hand thrown shape pierced in the leather-hard state

List of suppliers (U.K.)

Clays
Watts, Blake Bearne Ltd, Newton Abbot, Devon
Potclays Ltd, Copeland Street, Stoke-on-Trent

Raw materials and oxides
Podmore & Sons Ltd, Caledonian Mills, Shelton, Stoke-on-Trent

Prepared colours
Wengers Ltd, Etruria, Stoke-on-Trent
Matthey Blythe Ltd, Blythe Bridge, Creswell, Stoke-on-Trent

Pottery tools and brushes
Alec Tiranti Ltd, 72 Charlotte Street, London W1
Wengers Ltd, Etruria, Stoke-on-Trent
Podmore & Sons Ltd, Caledonian Mills, Shelton, Stoke-on-Trent

Kilns (electric)
Kilns & Furnaces Ltd, Keele Street Works, Turnstall, Stoke-on-Trent
Cromatie Kilns Ltd, Dividy Road, Longton, Stoke-on-Trent

Kiln furniture
Acme Marls Ltd, Clough Street, Hanley, Stoke-on-Trent

Wheels
Potters Equipment Co., 73–77 Britannia Road, London SW6

Cold wax resist
Technical Art Products, 202 Turnpike Link, East Croydon, Surrey

Booksellers
Drummond, 30 Hart Grove, Ealing Common, London W5
Tiranti Ltd, 72 Charlotte Street, London W1

List of suppliers (U.S.A.)

Clays, tools, and a complete line of equipment for the pottery maker

American Art Clay Co. Inc., 4717 West 16th Street, Indianapolis, Indiana

L. H. Butcher Co., 15th and Vermont Streets, San Francisco, California

Stewart Clay Co. Inc., 133 Mulberry Street, New York, New York

Jack D. Wolfe Co. Inc., 724 Meeker Avenue, Brooklyn, New York

Wheels and kilns

J. T. Abernathy, 212 South State Street, Ann Arbor, Michigan

A. D. Alpine, Inc., 11837 Teale Street, Culver City, California

American Art Clay Co., 4717 West 16th Street, Indianapolis, Indiana

Craftools, Inc., 401 Broadway, New York, New York

Randall Wheel, Box 531, Alfred, New York

Chemical oxides

L. H. Butcher Co., 15th and Vermont Streets, San Francisco, California

Jack D. Wolfe Co. Inc., 724 Meeker Avenue, Brooklyn, New York

For additional information on suppliers for the pottery maker, consult:

Research and Education Department, American Craftsmen's Council, 29 West 53rd Street, New York, New York

For further reading

Pottery: the Technique of Throwing by John Colbeck; Batsford, London and Watson-Guptill, New York

A Potter's Book by Bernard Leach; Faber, London and Transatlantic, Levittown, New York

The Technique of Pottery by D. M. Billington; Batsford, London

Clays and Glazes for the Potter by Daniel Rhodes; Pitman, London and Chilton, Philadelphia

Understanding Pottery Glazes by David Green; Faber, London

Stoneware and Porcelain by Daniel Rhodes; Pitman, London and Chilton, Philadelphia

Practical Pottery and Ceramics by Kenneth Clark; Studio Vista, London and Viking, New York

Simple Pottery by Kenneth Drake; Studio Vista, London and Watson-Guptill, New York

Index